LITTLE BOOK OF
HANGOVERS

Quentin Parker

THE LITTLE BOOK OF HANGOVERS

Copyright © Summersdale Publishers Ltd, 2015

Research by Sophie Martin

Illustrations © Shutterstock

Summersdale Publishers Ltd
46 West Street
Chichester
West Sussex
PO19 1RP
UK

www.summersdale.com

Printed and bound in the Czech Republic

ISBN: 978-1-84953-731-5

Substantial discounts on bulk quantities of Summersdale books are available to corporations, professional associations and other organisations. For details contact Nicky Douglas by telephone: +44 (0) 1243 756902, fax: +44 (0) 1243 786300 or email: nicky@summersdale.com.

Contents

Introduction

It's the morning after the night before – even though you said you were only going to have one cheeky pint – and your body feels like it's been trampled on by a million hangover gremlins. You can barely make it out of bed to be sick but, behold, there is a light at the end of this alcohol-induced tunnel. Packed with tests to gauge how drunk you are, hangover remedies and recipes, this book will help you to survive the shakes, sweats and shame (until the next time).

NB: There are deliberate spelling mistakes throughout this book. If you miss them, it probably means you're still hungover; if you don't, please put down the phone as I've already had to face the wrath of a number of pedants.

IF THIS DOG DO YOU BITE, SOON AS OUT OF YOUR BED, TAKE A HAIR OF THE TAIL THE NEXT DAY.

SCOTTISH PROVERB

BEFORE THE HANGOVER

The ultimate drinking game

RING OF FIRE

If you're chilling with friends and drinking at a medium pace but want to up the level of your antics, this is just the game to get you in the mood. I'm sure you've all played this drinking game before but below are some ready-made rules for Ring of Fire in case you are lacking the inspiration (or you're already too drunk) to make them up. Some require more drinking than others – it's up to you, the responsible adults, to decide the path you take and the intensity of the hangover you will have the next day. All you need is a pack of cards and the alcohol of your choice.

STANDARD RULES

(As a rule of thumb you should take two fingers' worth of drink when told to 'drink', but this can differ depending on how drunk you want to get.)

Ace is for waterfall – drink from when the person to your right starts drinking and stop drinking as soon as they stop drinking theirs.

2 is for you – choose a friend to drink.

3 is for me – you drink.

4 is for floor – last person to touch the floor drinks.

5 is for guys – men drink.

6 is for chicks – women drink.

7 is for heaven – last person to point to the sky drinks.

8 is for mate – the person who drew the card picks a person to drink with them every time they have to. The rule is passed on when the next person picks up an eight.

9 is for rhyme – take turns to go round the circle saying a word that rhymes with the previous one. Game stops and player drinks if the intended rhyme is unrhymed or the player takes more than 5 seconds to think of one.

10 is for never have I ever – each player starts clutching their drink with three fingers showing. The card dealer must begin a sentence with 'never have I ever...' and complete it with something they have never done. If the other players have done the thing, they must release one finger from their cup. The person to the card dealer's right then repeats this and play continues until the first player or players with no remaining fingers, who have done the most things, must drink.

Jack is make a rule – can be anything from no first names to no swearing; if a player breaks the rule they must drink. Rules are retracted when a new rule is made.

Queen is for question master – whoever picks up the card gets to ask other people questions, but they cannot answer them. If they do, they must drink.

King is for King's Cup – Each person who picks up a King must decant their drink to fill a quarter of the empty glass which is in the middle of the circle. Whoever draws the last King must fill the last quarter of the glass with their drink and down it.

OTHER RULES YOU CAN MIX AND MATCH TO VARY THE GAME

5 is for jive – the person who picked up the card does a dance move, which the person next to them must imitate and then add their own move. This is repeated until someone forgets the sequence, and they must then drink.

Joker is for gentlemen's rules – there should be only one Joker in the ring and when it's dealt everyone must stick to these rules: no first names, no pointing, prohibited to say 'drink', no swearing, no drinking with the hand you write with. Each time the rules are broken, that player must drink.

8 is for snake eyes – whoever picks up this card turns into one of Medusa's snakes; the only difference is whoever looks at them must drink (sorry, you won't be able to turn them to stone unfortunately). The person who dealt the eight loses their snake eyes powers once someone else picks up another eight.

6–10 is for green man – whoever picks up a card from six to ten is given the job of looking after an imaginary green man who sits on top of their glass. Whenever that person goes to drink they must take him off the glass and then put him back on once they have sipped/gulped their beverage. If they forget, they must drink again (remembering to take him off this time!).

MERRY OR MORTAL

How drunk are you?

TEST ONE:

THE DRNUK-O-METER – FIVE STAGES TO DRUNKEN UNENLIGHTENMENT

While you are still relatively sober, familiarise yourself with the stages of drunkenness you are likely to experience during the night:

CONFIDENCE: ☐ YES ☐ NO

Getting louder is a sure sign you are on your way to drunkdom. Go on, have another one...

DANCE WALKING: ☐ YES ☐ NO

Wanting to dance instead of walk to your intended destination is a sure sign of alcohol taking over, but remember from here on it's a slippery slope between getting merrier and just getting more pissed.

ASSERTIVENESS: ☐ YES ☐ NO

Becoming more vocal with your opinions and confiding
to strangers that you'd give the **PM** a run for their money
is one sign that you are switching from a happy drunk to
a raging lunatic. Advice is to lay off the vodka for a while.

GETTING WEIRD: ☐ YES ☐ NO

Meeting new people and immediately expressing your
love for them is a big indication that you have passed the
tipsy stage and are fast approaching stalker mode. Did
anyone tell you that doing this is really **NOT** cool?

NEAR PARALYSIS: ☐ YES ☐ NO

If you're stumbling around in the vain attempt to dance
while you still have smears of dried sick around your
mouth, then take yourself to bed (or ask a responsible
adult to carry you there).

TEST TWO:

BLURERD VISION –
HOW CLEARLY CAN YOU SEE?

Decipher each letter and unjumble them to make a word
describing your state:

TEST THREE:

THE SEARHCWORD — IS YOUR BRAIN STILL FUNCTIONING?

Find the following words in the puzzle below and prove yourself sober, or not:

BLADDERED

TIPSY

SLOSHED

LEGLESS

BLOTTO

X	A	N	N	Z	L	O	K	Z	C
S	E	S	L	O	S	H	E	D	H
C	V	Q	T	V	M	X	C	N	N
B	L	A	D	D	E	R	E	D	T
N	E	X	T	U	L	X	G	Z	I
N	G	Y	I	A	X	D	E	Y	P
K	L	D	X	Q	B	C	H	U	S
D	E	K	X	U	E	B	M	O	Y
G	S	I	H	L	P	W	W	G	Z
H	S	V	B	L	O	T	T	O	A

NEXT TO MUSIC, BEER WAS BEST.

CARSON McCULLERS

TEST FOUR:

TONGUE-TWITSERS – ARE YOU STARTING TO SLUR YOUR WORDS?

Say the following tricky words and tongue-twisters, repeating the tongue-twisters twice each. If you can chant them in a reasonable time without slurring or hiccupping, you shouldn't suffer too much the next day (that's if things don't go wildly wrong from here onwards).

TRICKY WORDS:

PRELIMINARY

LOQUACIOUS

MILLENNIUM

UNEQUIVOCAL

FUZZY DUCK, DUCKY FUZZ, FUZZY DUCK, DUCKY FUZZ

TONGUE-TWISTERS:

One smart fellow; he felt smart.
Two smart fellows; they felt smart.
Three smart fellows; they all felt smart.

A skunk sat on a stump.
The stump thought the skunk stunk.
The skunk thought the stump stunk.
What stunk, the skunk or the stump?

I am not the pheasant plucker,
I'm the pheasant plucker's mate.
I am only plucking pheasants
Because the pheasant plucker's late.

ALWAYS DO SOBER WHAT YOU SAID YOU'D DO DRUNK. THAT WILL TEACH YOU TO KEEP YOUR MOUTH SHUT.

ERNEST HEMINGWAY

TEST FIVE:

DRUNKEN DOT-TO-DOT — TEST YOUR HAND—EYE COORDNIATION

Focus your mind and complete the following dot-to-dots.
(If you're feeling hard-core, try spinning round three
times before you start.)

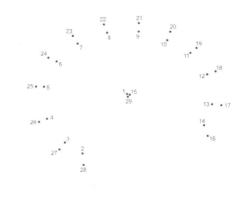

I WILL NEVER
DRINK AGAIN

IN WINE THERE IS WISDOM, IN BEER THERE IS FREEDOM, IN WATER THERE IS BACTERIA.

BENJAMIN FRANKLIN

THE
HANGOVERS

Which type do you have?

The
BASIC

OFTEN CAUSED BY ONE CHEEKY PINT DOWN THE PUB ON A SCHOOL NIGHT, WHICH IS INEVITABLY FOLLOWED BY A COUPLE MORE, THE BASIC HANGOVER IS COMPARABLE TO THE COMMON COLD. THE SYMPTOMS, WHICH INCLUDE MILD FOOD CRAVINGS, DROWSINESS AND SLOW REATCIONS, ARE BY NO MEANS GOING TO IMPACT ON WHAT YOU DO THE NEXT DAY BUT THEY WILL AFFECT HOW YOU DO THEM. WITH A LINGERING FUZZINESS OF THE BRAIN, YOUR ABILITY TO PERFORM THE EASIEST OF TASKS WILL DECREASE BY AROUND 30 PER CENT.

How to Cure

You will most likely epxerience the basic on a day of work/uni (when you actually have it). Here are some precautionary tips to help you through long meetings or seminars when, even on a good day, those buzzwords and acronyms go straight over your head.

1 Don't feel sorry for yourself; this could lead you to say something hurtful to a colleague in order to make yourself feel better.

2 Do something physical; whether it's running because you're late for work or lifting some weights at six in the morning, do some moderate exercise that'll make you slightly perspire. This will help to get rid of the nasty toxins in your bloodstream and to clear your mind. You may even find you are more productive at work than ever but don't take this as an excuse to get drunk every night!

3 Keep hydrated; water will suffice for this type of hangover.

HANGOVERS ARE A VIVID FORM OF VENGEANCE.

LIZ JENSEN

The
'I'M STILL
DRUNK'

IT'S 7 A.M., THE BIRDS ARE SINGING AND YOU ARE SINGING WITH THEM. BUT HOW, YOU WONDER, IS THIS POSSIBLE WHEN JUST FOUR HOURS AGO YOU WERE SINGING NOT THE BIRD'S SONG BUT THE BIRDIE SONG IN THE KEBAB SHOP AS YOU SHOVED BROWN SRTIPS OF UNKNOWN MEAT DOWN YOUR THROAT. THIS, MY FRIEND, IS BECAUSE YOU ARE STILL DRUNK. WHILE YOUR MATES ARE MOURNING THEIR VERY SOULS IN A LAST-DITCH ATTEMPT TO MAKE THEMSELVES FEEL BETTER THROUGH THE ART OF SELF-PITY, SEIZE THE DAY AND CARPE DIEM YOUR WAY THROUGH THE REST OF THE MORNING – IT WON'T BE LONG UNTIL YOU STOP SEIZING THE DAY, AND THE DAY, I.E. THE HANGOVER, STARTS SEIZING YOU.

How to Cure

Rather than cure this non-hangover, these steps will act more as a preventative – you might be able to escape it, you might not.

1 Be positive – although it's not a proven aid, a lot of the time we feel worse because we feel sorry for ourselves. So turn that frown upside down because a happy mind could make all the difference.

2 Dose yourself up on sports drink if you feel lethargic, as it will help you feel more alert for the day – but make sure you drink it in moderation.

3 Eat a banana – they are gentle on the stomach, therefore less likely to make a reappearance, good for boosting your blood sugar and contain lots of potassium, which will help you feel less dehydrated.

HOW DO I FEEL TODAY? I FEEL AS UNFIT AS AN UNFIDDLE.

OGDEN NASH

The MULTIPLE DAYER

UNLIKE WHEN YOU WERE A FRESH-FACED 18-YEAR-OLD AND DRINKING YOUR OWN BODY WEIGHT IN ALCOHOL DIDN'T REALLY FAZE YOU, THERE ARE HANGOVERS IN YOUR LATER YEARS THAT WILL FEED OFF YOUR MIND, BODY AND SOUL FOR THE BEST PART OF 48 HOURS. SYMPTOMS ARE FEELING LIKE A LESSER YOU, OR SOMEONE ELSE WHO ISN'T QUITE AS GOOD, AND SPORADIC FEELINGS OF MILD DEPRESSION AND TIREDNESS. WHEN THIS SIGNIFICANT MOMENT ARRIVES YOU MIGHT WANT TO START CONSIDERING ONLY DRINKING FRIDAYS INSTAED OF SATURDAYS IN ORDER TO DISPEL ANY CHANCE OF FEELING WORSE FOR WEAR WHEN YOU'RE BACK AT WORK ON MONDAY.

How to Cure

Obviously these solutions won't work straightaway as you will only know on day two if you are going to be hungover again, but they will help you to kick any residual yuckiness out of your system.

1 Drink a super detox smoothie on the first day of your hangover – find out how to make this on p.80.

2 Don't drink in an attempt to cure yourself with the 'hair of the dog'; it only stops the hangover for a while and by the next morning you'll feel even worse.

3 If you're reading this after you've drunk a gallon of cheap white cider, tough luck, but try to drink alcohol that isn't from the basic range of your local supermarket (yes, I'm speaking to the students out there). As well as tasting like something from a bottle underneath your kitchen sink, the stuff has added congeners (chemicals produced in the fermentation process which are poisonous) and sugar (which speeds up the depletion of vitamins). There are also fewer steps taken in the purifciation process.

DRINKING IS AN EMOTIONAL THING... IT YANKS YOU OUT OF YOUR BODY AND YOUR MIND AND THROWS YOU AGAINST THE WALL.

CHARLES BUKOWSKI

The
HEADBANGER

THIS HANGOVER IS PRETTY EASY TO
SELF-DIAGNOSE AS THE OVERRIDING
SYMPTOM CAN ONLY BE DESCRIBED AS
THE MOST EXCRUCIATING, SPLITTING
HEADACHE YOU'VE EVER EXPERIENCED.
USUALLY A SIGN THAT YOU DIDN'T HAVE
ENOUGH WATER BEFORE AND DURING
YOUR BENDER, THE DEHDYRATION WILL
MAKE YOUR BRAIN FEEL LIKE IT'S
SHRIVELLED UP TO THE SIZE OF A PEA.

With the feeling of utter hopelessness lingering over your head, you will want to get rid of this hangover straighatway.

1 Eat lots of water-rich fruit and vegetables, such as watermelon, papaya, cucumber and celery, as studies suggest that they work twice as effectively as a glass of water.

2 That's not to say you don't have to drink water now you've had your hydration elixir; ensure that you drink it throughout the day to keep your body topped up. If you're loath to drink water when you're hung-over, add some squash to give it a better taste and pop some ice cubes in to make it more refreshing. Or, to let you in on a little secret, you might want to try coconut milk, which has been dubbed the ultimate morning-after remedy.

HER HEAD FELT LIKE ELEPHANTS WERE DOING THE MERENGUE ON HER CEREBELLUM.

SUSAN FANETTI

The
UNFORGETTABLE

THIS HANGOVER WILL ALWAYS BE UNFORGETTABLE BECAUSE OF THE VERY FACT THAT YOU CAN'T REMEMBER A THING. YOU WILL INSTANTLY KNOW IF YOU HAVE THIS HANGOVER WHEN YOU WAKE UP AND WONDER HOW YOU GOT HOME ('HOME' IN THE BROADEST SENSE OF THE WORD, ANYWAY). THE MAIN SYPMTOM IS ANXIOUSNESS BUT, DEPENDING ON HOW YOU DEAL WITH THE ANXIETY, COULD DEVELOP INTO A JITTERY FEELING IN THE GUT.

How to Cure

Don't waste your day crying over what might have happened and take heed of some of the following advice.

1 Try not to sit by your computer all day flicking onto Facebook every other minute to check if you have any new notifications that refer to what happened the night before. This will only make the sick feeling in your stomach worse. What is done is done and if the events were worse than you thuoght they'd be, there's always the opportunity to move city or country.

2 If you think you'll feel better ringing your friend to get the low-down on what happened, don't put it off. The images you have dreamed up in your head probably surpass what really transpired; you might believe you led a heist but really the biggest news was that you showed off your signature moves in a dance-off.

THE LOVELY EFFECTS OF CHAMPAGNE WERE QUITE GONE AND ONLY THE NASTY ONES WERE LEFT.

MONICA DICKENS

The SPINNER

YOU'VE BEEN TO THE PUB AND IN A VERY SHORT SPACE OF TIME HAVE DRUNK MORE THAN YOU CAN REMEMBER. AS YOU STUMBLE HOME, THERE'S SOMETHING CREEPING UP ON YOU BUT IT'S NOT A PERSON; IT'S YOUR HANGOVER WAITING TO GRAPPLE WITH YOU WHEN YOU GET INDOORS. SYMPTOMS ARE PHSYICAL INABILITY TO LIE DOWN WITHOUT FEELING DIZZY/SICK, PHYSICAL INABILITY TO CLOSE YOUR EYES WITHOUT FEELING DIZZY/SICK, PHYSICAL INABILITY TO STAND UP STRAIGHT WITHOUT FEELING DIZZY/SICK.

How to Cure

Although it's a pain that you've just got back home from a good night out and you feel awful, it is more likely that you will have a less severe hangover in the monring if you adhere to the following steps straightaway.

1 Although one does not condone unhealthy eating at odd times, one of the best things you can do to help yourself is to munch your way through some carbs. This will help to absorb the drink.

2 Breathe in – one, two, three, four, five – and breathe out – one, two, three, four, five. By keeping your breathing steady and by paying attention to it you will take the focus off feeling dizzy.

FIRST YOU TAKE A DRINK, THEN THE DRINK TAKES A DRINK, THEN THE DRINK TAKES YOU.

F. SCOTT FITZGERALD

The
SOUL-
SUCKER

WHEN YOU STRUGGLE TO OPEN YOUR EYES AT THREE IN THE AFTERNOON AND SPEND THE REST OF THE DAY (WHAT LITTLE YOU HAVE LEFT) WITH YOUR HEAD IN THE TOILET, HAVING CRAWLED FROM THE BEDROOM TO GET THERE, THEN YOU KNOW THAT YOU HAVE ENTERED THE HANGOVER TWILIGHT ZONE. THE BEST ADVICE FOR THIS SITUATION IS TO AVOID THINKING, SPEAKING, LISTENING AND MOVING AND ACECPT THAT WHAT'S LEFT OF THE DAY IS A WRITE-OFF.

How to Cure

From the heading of this section you may be thinking
that there could be a chance of coming out the other side
of this hangover feeling fresh and invigorated, but this is
not the case and I must apologise profusely for dishing
out false hpoes. It is only that the heading must be used
in order for the pages to look orderly and consistent so
if you want to blame anyone blame aesthetics. Instead of
cures, all I can offer is some moral support and ways to
get the care and attention you so desperately need.

1 Think ahead and tactically; if you organise a big night
out when the chances of getting this hangover are
high make sure someone who would be happy to be your
carer (housemates might not be your best bet) is home
the next day. This ensures that you receive frequent
liquid top-ups, have someone to go out to the shop for
snacks and are given a bucket if it gets bad.

2 Sleep, eat, sleep, repeat (for the rest of the entire
day and night); your body will thank you for it.

HE LAY SPRAWLED,
TOO WICKED TO MOVE,
SPEWED UP LIKE A
BROKEN SPIDER-CRAB ON
THE TARRY SHINGLE
OF MORNING.

KINGSLEY AMIS

THE MYTHS

Remedies and red herrings

TO PREVENT OR CURE A HANGOVER
WE ARE TOLD TO HAVE A FRY-UP AND
DRINK MORE ALCOHOL THE NEXT DAY.
WE'RE ALSO TOLD TO TAKE HEED OF THE
ORDER IN WHICH WE DRIKN DIFFERENT
ALCOHOLS ON THE NIGHT. WHILE A
FRY-UP MAY TICK THE RIGHT BOXES,
EVEN IF THEY AREN'T THE SCIENTIFIC
ONES, A LOT OF WHAT YOU HEAR ABOUT
HANGOVER REMEDIES IS FALSE. THIS
CHAPTER SHOWS YOU WHICH ADVICE
IS TRUE AND WHICH IS NOT.

SPIRITS TO BEER – NEVER FEAR

MYTH

Although there is some truth in this, it's got nothing to do with what's different about the two drinks' ingredients, as you often hear. In fact, it's really down to the voulme of the drink and how much you consume. For instance, if you start off drinking singles with mixer and follow with pints of beer, you'll drink less of the latter, as it's a heavier drink and more likely to make you feel bloated, meaning that your intake slows down.

H₂O, ALCOHOL, H₂O, ALCOHOL

TRUE

When you've gone down to the pub for a few drinks, the main thing on your mind is alcohol. But if you know it's going to be a heavy one, drinking water in between your 'real' drinks will help reduce (but not cure) your hangover symptoms. You may not get as sluaghtered as you usually do but you'll certainly feel better for it in the morning.

WINE IS FINE

MYTH

Certain wines, especially red, contain a large amount of tannins and sulphites, which are known to cause headaches. But there is a glimmer of hope for the winos out there, as sulphite-free wine is available in most supermarkets, although slightly more expensive than your average sulphite-loaded wine. Whiskies and other malt drinks are also bad for heaadche hangovers. Drinks that are known to be gentler are beer and clear spirits.

HO! HO! HO!
TO THE BOTTLE I GO
TO HEAL MY HEART AND
DROWN MY WOE.

J. R. R. TOLKIEN

WOMEN AND MEN SUFFER THE SAME

MYTH

Those women who like to drink their male friends/
partner under the table will probably still be under
the table the next day while the man is out and about.
Because women store more fat in their bodies, which
doesn't absorb alcohol, this means more alcohol flows
through their bloosdtream, making them feel more
drunk that night and more hung-over the next day.

HONEY WILL MAKE YOU FEEL SUNNY – AND LEMONS TOO

TRUE

Studies suggest that honey is good for hangovers because it contains fructose, which helps speed up the breakdown of the alcohol. Lemon is said to be conducive to a faster recovery time as it has alkaline properties which help restore balacned pH levels in the body. So while you're having a pint of water the day after, try adding some honey or a slice of lemon to it.

COFFEE WILL MAKE YOU FEEL DANDY

MYTH

When you wake up, bleary-eyed, and reach for the kettle, think again before you have your dose of coffee, or anything with lots of caffiene in for that matter. If consumed in relatively large amounts, it makes you even more dehydrated and could end up making you feel worse. Instead, if you want something hot, try some herbal tea as it is known to relieve nausea and is packed with antioxidants, vitamins and minerals.

PAINKILLERS FOR PREVENTION

MYTH

Popping pills when you're drunk isn't good for anything and won't make your hangover subside the next day as the effects would have worn off by then. Instead take a couple of aspirins in the morning, an hour before you need to start functoining.

SLEEP TIGHT IN DAYLIGHT

TRUE

Sleeping when it's specifically daytime won't help cure a hangover but sleeping as much as possible the next day will help make you feel better. Although we tend to 'crash' when we've had too much to drink, our actual sleep is disrupted by our body's attempt at breaking down the alcohol. You are permitted to have as many power naps the next day as you like!

ONE MORE DRINK AND I'LL BE UNDER THE HOST.

MAE WEST

SWEAT IT OUT IN THE SAUNA

MYTH

You might think sweating the alcohol out through your skin is a quick fix to cure a hangover but think again as it could potentially be very dangerous. Because you're already very dehydrated your body will go into shock as you quickly launch yourself into extremley sweaty conditions. As well as this, it can damage blood vessels and disrupt your normal blood flow.

SWEAT IT OUT DOING EXERCISE

TRUE

Exercise is good for a hangover if taken in moderation and at the right time. As your body will feel fragile, don't go setting your alarm for 7 a.m. to get in that early morning 10 k but do (if you have the motiavtion) try going for a brisk walk or leisurely bike ride (that's if you're not still over the limit) after lots of water and some food. The fresh air will do wonders too.

THE RECIPES

Food to make you feel good

NO-STRESS FARMHOUSE FRY-UP

(SERVES THREE)

This one is good if you don't want much washing-up.

INGREDIENTS

4 TSP OLIVE OIL
300 G SLICED, PARBOILED POTATOES
250 G SLICED MUSHROOMS
100 G SPINACH, TORN
3 EGGS

OPTIONAL

PAPRIKA
PARMESAN OR CHEDDAR CHEESE, GRATED
BAGUETTE, TORN INTO PIECES

1 Warm 2 tsp oil in a pan, add the potatoes and sauté for 4–5 minutes over a medium heat, until browned.

2 Remove from heat and decant potatoes into a bowl.

3 Add another 2 tsp oil to the pan, along with the mushrooms and place the pan with the lid on over a medium heat for 5 minutes. Remove lid, turn up the heat and fry until the mushrooms are browned and there is no liquid.

4 Put the potatoes back in and add the spinach, sauté for 3 minutes, then break in 3 eggs. Replace lid and cook until the eggs have just set.

5 Season with a sprinkle of paprika and top with the baguette, if you like, and serve with the Parmesan or Cheddar.

PLAIN AND SIMPLE PORRIDGE

(SERVES ONE)

If your tummy's feeling a little delicate, try this safe but still super tasty option.

INGREDIENTS

50 G PORRIDGE OATS
350 ML MILK

TO SERVE

2 TBSP GREEK YOGURT, THINNED WITH A
    LITTLE MILK
HONEY

1 Combine the oats and milk in a large microwave-proof bowl, then microwave on high for 5 minutes, stirring halfway through. Leave to stand for 2 minutes.

2 Pour into a bowl, spoon yogurt on top and drizzle with honey.

I'D RATHER HAVE A BOTTLE IN FRONT OF ME THAN A FRONTAL LOBOTOMY.

ANONYMOUS

PROTEIN-PACKED PASTA
(SERVES TWO)

If you've missed breakfast you can always lean on this dish to start your day and give you a well-needed energy boost.

INGREDIENTS

3 TBSP OLIVE OIL
2 CHICKEN BREASTS, DICED
3 RASHERS BACON, CHOPPED
1 GARLIC CLOVE, CRUSHED
SALT AND FRESHLY GROUND BLACK PEPPER
150 ML DOUBLE CREAM
250 G FARFALLE

TO SERVE

100 G CHEDDAR OR PARMESAN CHEESE, GRATED
HANDFUL FRESH BASIL, TORN

1 Heat the oil in a frying pan, add the chicken and bacon and cook on a medium-high heat until the chicken is golden-brown and cooked through.

2 Add the garlic and cook for 1 minute. Season with salt and freshly ground black pepper, then add the cream and keep on a low heat.

3 While frying the chicken and bacon, cook the pasta according to packet instructions in a pan of salted boiling water, then drain.

4 Add the creamy chicken and bacon mixture to the cooked, drained pasta and stir well.

5 Serve and garnish with cheese and basil.

SUPER DETOX SMOOTHIE
(SERVES TWO)

Yes, it might be green and, yes, it might not look dissimilar to what has already come up this morning, but this smoothie will help you recover from the deadliest of hangovers.

INGREDIENTS

1 CUP MIXED BERRIES, FROZEN
½ CUP PINEAPPLE, PAPAYA OR MANGO, DICED
1 CUP DANDELION GREENS
½ CUP SPINACH
½ CUP COCONUT MILK
1–1 ½ CUP COCONUT WATER

1 Place all the ingredients into a blender.

2 Blend until mixed thoroughly.

3 Pour into a glass and drink slowly, so you savour
the taste and your body can absorb the nutrients.

DELICIOUSLY SMOOTH SMOOTHIE

(SERVES ONE)

If you are put off by how healthy the detox smoothie sounds (although mark my words it tastes marvellous) try this instead.

INGREDIENTS

1 WHOLE LARGE RIPE BANANA
1 ½ CUP MILK
2 TBSP HONEY

 Place all three ingredients into a blender.

 Blend until smooth.

 Pour into a glass and make a toast to getting rid of your hangover.

CHICKEN NOODLES

(SERVES TWO)

Nutritious, wholesome and hearty food – just what is
needed for a hangover.

INGREDIENTS

1 TBSP OLIVE OIL
4 CHICKEN BREASTS, DICED
1 GARLIC CLOVE, CRUSHED OR SLICED
1 RED PEPPER, THINLY SLICED
1 GREEN PEPPER, THINLY SLICED
5 SPRING ONIONS, SLICED
100 G BEAN SPROUTS
2 X 150 G PACKS DRY NOODLES
3 TBSP OYSTER SAUCE

1 Heat the oil in a large frying pan, then stir-fry the chicken until golden and cooked all the way through.

2 Mix in the garlic and pepper and cook for 2 minutes, then add the spring onions, bean sprouts, noodles, sauce and 5 tbsp water and stir-fry everything for another 2 minutes. Serve immediately.

ULTIMATE BEANS ON TOAST
(SERVES TWO)

A classic recipe with a twist and can be made on all levels of a hangover because it's so simple.

INGREDIENTS

2 EGGS
4 SLICES OF BREAD, FRESH IS BEST
1 TBSP OLIVE OIL
1 ONION, DICED
½ TSP GROUND CUMIN
½ TSP GROUND CORIANDER
85 G SEMI-DRIED TOMATOES FROM A JAR,
   CHOPPED IF LARGE
400 G CAN BAKED BEANS
BUTTER, FOR SPREADING (OPTIONAL)

TO SERVE

FRESH CHOPPED CORIANDER OR PARSLEY
CUMIN

1 Bring water to the boil in a saucepan for the eggs and toast the bread. Heat the oil in a frying pan, then add the onion and gently cook for a few minutes until it starts to brown. Mix the spices into the pan and stir briefly. Add the tomatoes and beans and cook until warm through.

2 Turn down the heat under the saucepan so the water is just simmering, then crack in the eggs and gently poach them until the whites are firm but the yolks are still runny. Layer the beans onto the toast (buttered or unbuttered, as you wish) and place the eggs on top.

3 Serve with a sprinkle of extra cumin and coriander or parsley.

BANANA MUFFINS

(MAKES TEN)

Great for a boost of energy to start the day but it's advised to bake these cakes the day before so you can eat them first thing!

INGREDIENTS

75 G MELTED BUTTER
250 G SELF-RAISING FLOUR
I TSP BAKING POWDER
½ TSP BICARBONATE OF SODA
PINCH OF SALT
½ TSP GROUND CINNAMON
½ TSP GROUND NUTMEG
115 G CASTER SUGAR
I TSP VANILLA EXTRACT
2 LARGE, RIPE BANANAS
2 MEDIUM EGGS
125 ML MILK, FULL FAT
10 WALNUT KERNELS (OPTIONAL)

1 Heat the oven to 190°C/375°F/Gas mark 5. Melt the butter in the microwave and allow to cool. Mash the bananas and sift the flour, baking powder, bicarbonate of soda, salt, cinnamon and nutmeg together in a large bowl, then add caster sugar and stir well.

2 With a fork, beat together the eggs. Add the vanilla extract, melted butter and milk in a second bowl, adding the mashed banana after and stir through.

3 Make a well in the centre of the dry ingredients and add the egg mixture, stirring roughly with a fork until it is a lumpy paste.

Place paper cases into a cupcake tray and spoon in the mixture level with the tops of the cases. Add a walnut kernel to the top of each mixture, if you like.

Bake for 20 to 25 minutes or until the muffins come away from the side of the pan when touched. Rest the muffin tray on a wire rack for five minutes, then remove the muffins and leave on the rack for another five minutes to cool.

Store away until the following day, trying not to eat them all when you come in drunk.

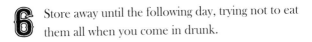

I DRINK TO MAKE OTHER PEOPLE MORE INTERESTING.

GEORGE JEAN NATHAN

CONCLUSION

Now you've learnt about the different hangovers and have tried every cure in this book – probably not a good idea to try them all at once – hopefully you can bear your hangover better than you did before. It's not always easy to confidently say that you'll drink again when you are suffering from the stuff that 12 hours before you were gagging for, but with a bit of luck this book will have appeased your fury at the common hangover and you'll be saying cheers sooner than you thought!

HAPPY HANGOVERS!

The

LITTLE BOOK OF

COCKTAILS

Rufus Cavendish

THE LITTLE BOOK OF
COCKTAILS

Rufus Cavendish

£5.99

Paperback

ISBN: 978-1-84953-585-4

Swap the drab for the dazzle with this concoction of moreish recipes and nifty tips that will equip you with everything you need to put the party back into cocktail. Shaken or stirred, flaming or fizzy, let the cocktail, whichever way you like it, be a part of any sparkling occasion.

The

LITTLE BOOK OF

DRINKING GAMES

Quentin Parker

THE LITTLE BOOK OF
DRINKING GAMES

Quentin Parker

£5.99

Paperback

ISBN: 978-1-84953-586-1

Liven up the party with this heady collection of drinking games! Choose from brain-boggling classics such as Fuzzy Duck and Slap, Clap, Click or dizzying games of chance like TV Drinking and Vodka Roulette – whichever you play, you're guaranteed to be gleeful and giggly by the end!

If you're interested in finding out more about our books, find us on Facebook at **SUMMERSDALE PUBLISHERS** and follow us on Twitter at **@SUMMERSDALE**.

WWW.SUMMERSDALE.COM